Event

News for every day ~~ ~~ ar

The official engagement portrait of the actor and future US President Ronald Reagan and Nancy Davis. They are married on 4 March 1952.

By Hugh Morrison

MONTPELIER PUBLISHING

Published in Great Britain by Montpelier Publishing.
This edition © 2021. All rights reserved.
ISBN: 9798741275320

January 1952

Tuesday 1: 62 people are killed in six separate air crashes across the USA.

Wednesday 2: The musical *Pal Joey* is revived on Broadway, eventually running for 542 performances.

Johnnie Ray.

Thursday 3: The long running crime drama series *Dragnet* begins on US TV.

Friday 4: An enormous explosion takes place on the Channel Island of Herm, when a floating mine dating from the Second World War hits the town harbour in stormy weather. None of the island's 28 residents is harmed.

Saturday 5: British Prime Minister Winston Churchill arrives in the USA for talks with President Truman.

Sunday 6: *Cry* by Johnnie Ray enters the second week of an eleven week run at the top of the US singles charts.

January 1952

Winston Churchill and Harry S Truman confer in the White House, 5 January.

Monday 7: Controversial West German plans to set up a new army under the control of former Wehrmacht officers are revealed.

Tuesday 8: US President Truman announces in his State of the Union Address that the victory over communism depends on 'whether the hungry can be fed.'

Wednesday 9: The freighter SS *Pennsylvania* sinks in north Pacific 465 miles off Vancouver Island; no trace of the 46 crew is found.

Thursday 10: The Cecil B De Mille-directed film *The Greatest Show on Earth*, starring Betty Hutton and Cornel Wilde, premieres in New York City.

Friday 11: West Germany's parliament ratifies the Schuman Plan on European trade; the first move towards what becomes the European Union.

Saturday 12: The English sculptor Jessie Lipscomb, the first female student of Rodin, dies aged 90.

Sunday 13: US Supreme Court Justice William O Douglas warns of the 'black silence of fear' caused by anti-communist censorship.

Monday 14: The world's first informal morning TV talk show, *Today,* is broadcast on NBC in the USA.

Tuesday 15: Damage estimated at £1m is caused when severe storms hit Scotland's Orkney Islands.

Wednesday 16: 226 passengers are rescued after spending three days trapped on board an unheated express train snowed under by a blizzard near Lake Tahoe, California.

Sooty makes his first TV appearance on 16 January.

The glove puppet Sooty first appears on BBC TV, on *Talent Night*.

Thursday 17: The colour bar in PGA golf ends as boxer Joe Louis becomes the first black player in the San Diego Open.

Curly Howard.

Friday 18: The Three Stooges comedian Curly Howard dies aged 48.

Jawaharlal Nehru becomes Prime Minister of India on 21 January.

Saturday 19: Two people are killed and 193 injured when a footbridge collapses at Knowsley Street Station, Bury, Lancashire.

Sunday 20: Communist insurgents kill a Royal Marines Commando during an ambush in Perak, Malaya.

January 1952

A British soldier and native Egyptian police in a street battle in Ismailia, Egypt, 25 January.

Monday 21: Jawaharlal Nehru's Congress Party is victorious in India's first general election.

Tuesday 22: The French surrealist playwright Roger Vitrac dies aged 52.

Wednesday 23: The South African cricketer Omar Henry, the first non-white player since the introduction of apartheid, is born in Stellenbosch, Cape Province.

Thursday 24: Allied forces engage in a six hour battle with communist forces at Chorwon, Korea.

Friday 25: USAF fighters down ten communist Mig-15 planes in an aerial battle over northwest Korea.

Saturday 26: 'Black Saturday' in Egypt: anti-British rioters loot and burn businesses in central Cairo.

Sunday 27: Peace talks begin between Allied and communist forces in Korea.

Ken McGregor wins the Australia Men's Open tennis championships on 28 January.

Monday 28: Tennis star Ken McGregor wins the Australian Mens' Open.

Tuesday 29: Aly Maher Pasha takes over as premier of Egypt and declares martial law following anti-British rioting.

Wednesday 30: Korean War peace talks break down.

Thursday 31: HRH Princess Elizabeth arrives in Nairobi, Kenya, on a state visit.

Aly Maher Pasha (centre) becomes premier of Egypt on 29 January.

February
1952

Friday 1: The first 'TV detector van' goes into use in the UK in an attempt to crack down on unlicensed TV sets.

A general strike takes place in Tunisia in protest at French rule.

Saturday 2: The Groundhog Day Storm forms off the coast of Cuba.

Sunday 3: Korean War armistice talks resume in Tokyo, as Allied and communist forces clash in -15F temperatures near Seoul.

Monday 4: The evangelist Billy Graham preaches to a crowd of 45,000 from the steps of the Capitol in Washington, DC.

Tuesday 5: The Royal Navy sends the frigate HMS *Burghead Bay* to Antarctica after Argentinian explorers fire shots at British counterparts in disputed territory.

Wednesday 6: HM King George VI dies aged 56.

Left: HM the King.

February 1952

THE KING THE PEOPLE LOVED

THE QUEEN WHO IS OUR HOPE

We have said our last farewells to King George VI. Let us remember him not in sadness but in the spirit that he would himself have wished, putting grief behind us in the memory of his courage, his kindliness and his faith. These virtues that we loved in him live on unconquerably in his daughter, our Queen.

Above: newspaper report of the Accession.

Thursday 7: After some delay due to being in a remote safari lodge in Kenya, HRH Princess Elizabeth is informed of the death of her father the King.

Friday 8: HM Queen Elizabeth's accession is formally proclaimed on her return to England from Kenya.

Saturday 9: The novelist and travel writer Norman Douglas (*South Wind*) dies aged 83.

Sunday 10: Major George A Davis Jr, the highest-scoring American air ace of the Korean War, is shot down and killed near the Chinese border.

Monday 11: Pope Pius XII calls for a spiritual crusade in the face of western civilization's 'potential ruin'.

Tuesday 12: A queue of 100,000 people begins to file past the coffin of King George VI in Westminster Hall, London. Queen Mary the Queen Dowager and Edward, Duke of Windsor, (the former King Edward VIII) attend the vigil.

Above: Pope Pius XII.

February 1952

VI OLYMPIC WINTER GAMES

14-25 February 1952
OSLO - NORWAY

Poster for the Winter Olympics.

Wednesday 13: Rocky Marciano knocks out Lee Savold in Philadelphia to claim the World Heavyweight boxing title.

Thursday 14: The 1952 Winter Olympics begin in Oslo, Norway.

Friday 15: The funeral of HM King George VI takes place at St George's Chapel, Windsor Castle.

Saturday 16: Speed skater Ken Henry wins gold for the USA in the Oslo olympics.

Sunday 17: Heavy snowstorms hit the northeastern USA, with up to 30 inches of snow falling on New England.

Monday 18: The communist government of East Germany bans the reporting of suicides by the press.

Greece and Turkey join NATO.

Tuesday 19: US figure skater Dick Button becomes the first to land a triple jump in a competition, during the 1952 Winter Olympics in Norway.

Wednesday 20: Peace talks between British and Egyptian authorities in the Suez area are announced following severe rioting in January.

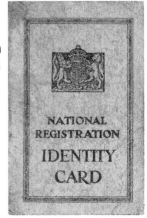

British identity cards are abolished on 21 February.

Thursday 21: Britain abolishes ID cards, introduced in 1939, following pressure from civi lliberties campaigners.

Friday 22: German husband and wife team Ria and Paul Falk win the mixed skating pairs gold medal at the Winter Olympics.

Saturday 23: The British boys' adventure comic *Lion* is first published.

Sunday 24: Canada wins its sixth olympic ice hockey title after tying 3-3 with the USA at the Winter Olympics.

Monday 25: The Winter Olympics ends.

Tuesday 26: Prime Minister Winston Churchill announces that Britain has developed an atomic bomb.

Wednesday 27: Britain's Parliament debates whether the new Queen should be officially styled 'Elizabeth the Second' or 'Elizabeth the First of Scotland and Second of England.' The former title is chosen.

Thursday 28: Vincent Massey is sworn in as the first Canadian-born Governor-General of Canada.

Friday 29: Britain's Lawrence Demmy and Jean Westwood win the Ice Dance World Championships in Paris.

Right: Lion comic for boys is first published on 23 February.

March
1952

Saturday 1: The island of Heligoland is returned to West Germany after being under British rule since 1945.

Sunday 2: The Piper PA23 light aircraft is first flown.

Monday 3: 38 people are killed when an Air France airliner crashes shortly after take-off at Nice airport.

Tuesday 4: The future US President Ronald Reagan marries Nancy Davis in Hollywood, California.

Wednesday 5: Five communist Mig-15 jets are shot down by USAF F-86 Sabre jets near the Yalu River, Korea.

The Piper PA23 is launched on 2 March.

Thursday 6: Cardiff shopkeeper Lily Volpert, 42, is killed during a robbery attempt. Mahmood Mattan, the chief suspect, becomes the last man to be hanged in Wales. In 1998 the Court of Appeal concludes he was wrongfully convicted.

Friday 7: *The New Musical Express* is first published in the UK. It goes on to publish the first singles charts in November 1952.

Saturday 8: The Royal Navy destroyer HMS *Daring* is commissioned.

General Batista seizes control of Cuba on 10 March.

Sunday 9: Heinz Neuhaus becomes European Heavyweight Boxing Champion.

Monday 10: General Fulgencio Batista re-takes control of Cuba in a military coup.

General the Lord Ismay becomes UN Secretary General on 12 March.

Tuesday 11: Douglas Adams, author of *The Hitchhiker's Guide to the Galaxy* is born in Cambridge, England (died 2001).

Wednesday 12: Britain's General the Lord Ismay DSO, Indian Army (Ret), becomes the first Secretary General of NATO.

Thursday 13: Severe bush fires destroy 5000 acres of forest in New South Wales, Australia.

Friday 14: Field Marshal Harold Alexander is created First Earl

March 1952

Alexander of Tunis for his service to the British Army in the Second World War.

Saturday 15: The rainiest day on record takes place, as 71.8 inches falls on Reunion Island in the Indian Ocean.

Humphrey Bogart (shown here with Katharine Hepburn) wins the Academy Award for Best Actor for *The African Queen* on 20 March.

Sunday 16: Phillipe Kahn, inventor of the camera phone, is born in Paris, France.

Monday 17: The thriller *Home at Seven* starring Ralph Richardson is released in the UK.

Tuesday 18: The Royal Navy's Home and Mediterranean fleets take part in large scale exercises around the colony of Malta.

Field Marshal Harold Alexander is created Earl of Tunis on 14 March.

Wednesday 19: A submarine volcano erupts in the Phillipines creating a 250 foot high new island 350 miles north of Manila.

Thursday 20: In the 24th Academy Awards, Humphrey Bogart wins Best Actor for *The African Queen*; Kim Hunter wins Best Actress for *A Streetcar Named Desire*.

Friday 21: 343 people are killed and $15m worth of damage is caused when tornadoes sweep across the southern states of the USA.

March 1952

Saturday 22: Wales defeats France 9-5 in the Five Nations Rugby tournament in Swansea.

Sunday 23: Bill Mosienko of the Chicago Blackhawks sets the record for the fastest ever ice-hockey hat-trick (21 seconds).

Monday 24: 'James Bond' author Ian Fleming marries Anne Charteris in Jamaica.

Cars travelling abroad are required to carry a country designation plate from 26 March.

Tuesday 25: Robbers escape with $600,000 during an armoured car robbery in Danvers, Massachusetts.

Singin' in the Rain **is released on 27 March.**

Wednesday 26: The Geneva Convention on Road Traffic comes into force, requiring cars travelling abroad to carry a three-letter country designation nameplate.

Thursday 27: The musical comedy *Singin' in the Rain* starring Gene Kelly is released.

A policeman is killed by a letterbomb intended to assassinate the Chancellor of West Germany, Konrad Adenauer.

Friday 28: The US Figure Skating Championships are won by Richard Button and Tenley Albright.

March 1952

USAF F-86 Sabre jet fighters in action over Korea, 1952.

Saturday 29: US President Harry S Truman announces he will not run for election again.

Sunday 30: 25 Allied jets are outnumbered by 70 communist aircraft during a major aerial battle west of Yonchon, Korea.

Monday 31: The computing pioneer Alan Turing is convicted of several counts of indecency in Manchester.

Actor Dermot Morgan (*Father Ted*) is born in Dublin (died 1998).

April
1952

Tuesday 1: The NATO Phonetic Alphabet (Alpha, Bravo, Charlie, etc) is adopted for civil aviation.

Wednesday 2: The British Parliament debates the use of collective punishment by troops in the Malayan Emergency.

Thursday 3: Newcastle United win football's FA Cup for the fifth time. It is the first Cup Final in which a foreigner (George Robledo) scores a goal.

Friday 4: 78 Norwegian seal hunters vanish without a trace from the West Ice, Greenland.

Lucille Ball and Desi Arnaz in *I Love Lucy*.

Saturday 5: Arthur Thompson wins the Grand National on Teal, with odds of 100-7.

Sunday 6: Sam Snead wins the second of his three US Masters titles at Augusta National Golf Club, Georgia.

Monday 7: The *I Love Lucy* episode *The Marriage License* is the confirmed as the first TV programme to be watched by 10,000,000 households.

April 1952

Stephen Seagal is born on 10 April.

Tuesday 8: The US Supreme Court limits the power of the President to seize private assets, following Truman's threat to nationalise the steel industry to avert a strike.

Wednesday 9: The Bolivian National Revolution takes place under leader Victor Paz Estenssoro.

Thursday 10: The action-film actor and martial arts expert Steven Seagal is born in Lansing, Michigan.

Friday 11: Good Friday. Communist troops seize Nanri Island from Chinese nationalist forces.

Saturday 12: King Norodom Sihanouk of Cambodia marries Paule Monique Izzi.

Sunday 13: Easter Sunday. Allied and communist forces in Korea make tentative efforts to resume peace talks.

The first test flight of the USAF B-52 bomber takes place on 15 April.

Monday 14: 74,000 people are made homeless after severe flooding of the Missouri River around Sioux City, Iowa.

Tuesday 15: The Boeing B-52 Stratofortress flies for the first time.

Wednesday 16: A major Allied air attack in North Korea cuts the railway lines used to supply communist troops in 52 locations.

Thursday 17: The USA's JC Penney department store chain celebrates its Golden Jubilee.

Friday 18: West Germany and Japan form diplomatic relations.

Saturday 19: Large crowds gather in New York City to see Queen Juliana of the Netherland's procession as part of her state visit to the USA.

HM Queen Juliana with President Truman.

Sir Stafford Cripps, former UK Chancellor, dies on 21 April.

Sunday 20: A major Allied naval bombardment of the North Korean coast begins as bad weather stops all land and air engagement.

Monday 21: Sir Stafford Cripps, prominent Labour MP and Chancellor of the Exchequer under Clement Atlee, dies aged 62.

Tuesday 22: The first nuclear test explosion to be televised takes place at Yucca Flats, Nevada.

Wednesday 23: One convict dies and $2.5m damage occurs during a prison riot in Jackson, Michigan.

April 1952

Jean-Paul Gaultier is born on 24 April.

Thursday 24: Fashion designer Jean Paul Gaultier is born in Arcueil, France.

Friday 25: The West German state of Baden-Württemberg is created out of two former Allied zones of occupation.

Saturday 26: The US Navy aircraft carrier USS *Wasp* collides with the destroyer USS *Hobson* during exercises in the Atlantic, with the loss of 175 men.

Sunday 27: Three people are killed when a USAAF jet of 165 Fighter Bomber Squadron crash lands in the village of St Peter's, Isle of Thanet, Kent.

Monday 28: The Treaty of San Francisco goes into effect, formerly ending the state of war between the USA and Japan and ending the American occupation of Japan.

Tuesday 29: Lever House, the first international style skyscraper, opens in New York City.

Britain's first post-war university, the University of Southampton, is established.

Wednesday 30: Mr Potato Head becomes the first toy to be advertised on US television.

Left: Lever House, New York City's first international style building, opens on 29 April.

May 1952

Thursday 1: 2150 US Marines are subjected to a live atom bomb test at Yucca Flats, Nevada. The soldiers, in trenches four miles from the explosion, are reported to be unharmed.

Friday 2: The world's first jet airliner, the deHavilland Comet, goes into service between London and Johannesburg.

Saturday 3: The first US explorers set foot on the geographic North Pole.

Sunday 4: British TV personality Michael Barrymore is born in London.

Monday 5: Herman Wouk's novel *The Caine Mutiny* is awarded the Pulitzer Prize for Literature.

Tuesday 6: The Italian educationalist Maria Montessori, founder of the Montessori System, dies aged 81.

US Marines observe the nuclear blast at Yucca Flats, Nevada, on 1 May.

May 1952

The first commercial passenger jet airliner, the de Havilland Comet, goes into service on 2 May.

Wednesday 7: British computer scientist Geoffrey Dummer publishes his proposals for integrated circuits, an essential component of modern computing.

Thursday 8: *The Lavender Hill Mob* starring Alec Guinness wins Best British Film in the British Academy Film Awards (BAFTAs).

Friday 9: The thriller film *The Sniper*, starring Adolph Menjou, which breaks new ground in its realistic depiction of a serial killer, is released.

Saturday 10: *Two Cents Worth of Hope* and *Othello* win joint Grand Prix in the 1952 Cannes Film Festival.

Sunday 11: Admiral the Earl Mountbatten takes over as commander in chief of Britain's Mediterranean Fleet.

Monday 12: Four year old Gaj Singh is crowned Maharajah of Jodhpur, following the sudden death of his father.

Tuesday 13: 11 die when a Corsair fighter collides with a USAF B29 bomber during a training exercise off the California coast.

Wednesday 14: The Italian composer Italo Montemezzi dies aged 76.

May 1952

South Korean navy guards at Pusan POW camp, where mutiny breaks out on 20 May.

Thursday 15: Gavesh Mavalankar becomes the first Speaker of the Indian parliament.

Friday 16: A major fire destroys much of the Warner Brothers film studios in Los Angeles.

Saturday 17: The British psychologist William Brown, a pioneer of shell-shock treatment, dies aged 71.

Sunday 18: British yachtswoman Ann Davison becomes the first woman to sail solo around the world.

Monday 19: 'Operation Roundup' takes place as Allied commandos, supported by the Royal Australian Navy, land at Ponggu Mon, Korea.

Tuesday 20: Communist prisoners of war mutiny at Pusan Camp, Korea.

Wednesday 21: The Eastcastle Street Robbery in London takes place; £287,000 is stolen from a post office van in the biggest post-war robbery to this date.

General Mark Clark.

Thursday 22: Four airmen are killed and seven injured when an RAF Lancaster bomber crashes near Maidstone, Kent.

Friday 23: UN forces commander Mark Clark demotes the officers in charge of the POW camp in Pusan, Korea, following the mutiny of 20 May.

May 1952

Saturday 24: Actress Joan Collins marries actor Maxwell Reed.

Sunday 25: The Soviet Union agrees to Allied talks on German reunification. Reunification does not happen until 1991.

Monday 26: The Bonn Convention is signed by the western Allies, who agree to end occupation of West Germany by 1955.

The world's smallest aeroplane to this date, the 9' Stits Sky Baby, is first flown in California.

The Stits Sky Baby, the world's smallest aeroplane, first flies on 26 May.

Tuesday 27: The Treaty of Paris is signed to form a pan-European army. France and Italy fail to ratify it, so the plan never comes to fruition.

Wednesday 28: Women in Greece win the right to stand for parliament.

Thursday 29: Tensions rise in Berlin as the East German government threatens to cut rail links with West Berlin. British Foreign Secretary Anthony Edens states 'any attack on West Berlin is an attack on the Western powers.'

Friday 30: General Dwight D Eisenhower hands over command of Allied forces in Europe to General Matthew D Ridgeway, in order to stand in the US Presidential election.

Saturday 31: Berlin goes on high alert as East German forces seize two outlying villages from the British and American sectors.

June
1952

Sunday 1: The Roman Catholic church bans the books of French author André Gide.

Prescription charges of one shilling are introduced in the United Kingdom.

Monday 2: A 53-day strike by US steelworkers begins.

Tuesday 3: 26,000 miners and 9000 railway workers are put on furlough as a knock-on effect of the US steel strike.

Wednesday 4: Tensions in Berlin continue to run high as a US patrol is shot at by Soviet forces.

Thursday 5: Jersey Joe Walcott retains boxing's World Heavyweight title when he beats Ezzard Charles in the USA's first nationally televised match. Zack Clayton also becomes the first world title black referee.

English cricketer Fred Trueman makes his Test debut.

Jersey Joe Walcott, World Heavyweight champion.

June 1952

Nguyễn Văn Tâm.

Friday 6: Nguyễn Văn Tâm becomes Prime Minister of Vietnam.

Saturday 7: Actor Liam Neeson is born in Ballymena, County Antrim.

Sunday 8: Actress Judy Garland marries producer Sidney Luft in Hollister, California.

Monday 9: The charity War on Want is launched in the UK.

Tuesday 10: 31 communist POWs and one American soldier are killed during a mutiny at the Koje prison camp in Korea.

Wednesday 11: Len Hutton is appointed as the first professional cricketer to captain England.

Thursday 12: The second Berlin International Film Festival begins.

Friday 13: An international incident known as the Catalina Affair takes place when two Swedish planes in international waters are shot down by Soviet fighters. The USSR denies responsibility until 1991.

Len Hutton.

Saturday 14: Myxomatosis is introduced to Europe in an attempt to cull rabbits on an estate in France.

Sunday 15: The first English translation of *Anne Frank's Diary* is published.

Liam Neeson.

Monday 16: A rescue plane searching for the Swedish planes shot down on 13 June also comes under Soviet fire and is forced to ditch.

Tuesday 17: Chrysler motors announces that the ongoing steel strike will hamper the production of vehicles and parts to supply US troops in Korea.

Wednesday 18: Actress Isabella Rossellini (*Blue Velvet*) is born in Rome, Italy.

Thursday 19: The long-running quiz show *I've Got A Secret* is first broadcast on CBS TV, presented by Garry Moore.

Friday 20: Actor John Goodman (*Roseanne*) is born in St Louis, Missouri.

Saturday 21: William Marshall, 24, a radio operator in Britain's Foreign Office, is charged with passing secrets to the Russians. He is later sentenced to five years in prison.

Sunday 22: Alberto Ascari wins the 1952 Belgian Grand Prix.

Host Garry Moore and panelist Hermione Gingrich on the US quiz show *I've Got A Secret*, which first airs on 19 June.

June 1952

Monday 23: The Indian cricket team meets HM Queen Elizabeth II at Lord's Cricket Ground, London, in its first visit to England since Independence.

Tuesday 24: Britain's Labour opposition party raises concerns in Parliament over the direction of the Korean War, following bombing of civilian targets.

Wednesday 25: Jim Turnesa wins the 1952 PGA golf championships at Louisville, Kentucky.

Thursday 26: The ANC (African National Congress) launches the Defiance Campaign, the first organised resistance to the apartheid laws in South Africa.

Friday 27: Test pilot Jean 'Skip' Zeigler performs the first test flight of the X-2 high speed rocket plane from Edwards Air Force base, California.

Saturday 28: Armi Kuusela of Finland wins the first Miss Universe beauty pageant, held in Long Beach, California.

Left: Miss Universe, Armi Kuusela.

Sunday 29: The USS *Oriskany* becomes the first aircraft carrier to round Cape Horn, being too large to navigate the Panama Canal.

Monday 30: The US radio soap opera *The Guiding Light*, first broadcast in 1937, makes the transition to TV.

July
1952

Dan Aykroyd.

Tuesday 1: Actor and comedian Dan Aykroyd is born in Ottawa, Canada.

Wednesday 2: Hussein Serri Pasha becomes Prime Minister of Egypt.

Thursday 3: The SS *United States* begins her maiden voyage; she is the largest American cruise liner and the fastest to cross the Atlantic.

Friday 4: Communist air forces suffer their worst day of losses in the Korean War, with 11 MiGs shot down by Allied fighters.

The **SS** *United States.*

July 1952

London's last tram runs on 6 July.

Saturday 5: Australia's Frank Sedgman and the USA's Maureen Connoly win the Wimbledon tennis championships.

Sunday 6: Cheering crowds turn out to greet the last of London's trams, as it makes its final journey from Woolwich to New Cross.

The novelist Hilary Mantel (*Wolf Hall*) is born in Glossop, Derbyshire.

Monday 7: Adolfo Ruiz Cortines becomes President of Mexico.

Tuesday 8: Lt DE Wood, one of the US Navy's Blue Angels aerobatics display team, is killed when his plane malfunctions during an air show at Corpus Christi, Texas.

Wednesday 9: West Berlin authorities blockade all roads into the Russian sector following the kidnapping of a leading anti-communist lawyer by East Berliners.

Thursday 10: 336 communist troops are reported dead after a major UN advance in Korea near Pyongyang.

Friday 11: South African golfer Bobby Locke wins the British Open at Lytham St Annes.

General Dwight D Eisenhower is nominated as the Republican candidate for the US Presidential elections.

Bobby Locke wins the British Open on 11 July.

Finnish runner Paavo Nurmi opens the Olympic Games on 19 July.

Saturday 12: A series of UFO sightings around Washington, DC over 17 days begins; the sightings are investigated by the USAF and CIA and later dismissed as false alarms.

Sunday 13: East Germany, disarmed since 1945, announces plans to create a new army.

Monday 14: The liner SS *United States* sets the world record for a westward Atlantic crossing at 84 hours, 12 minutes.

Celia Imrie is born on 15 July.

Tuesday 15: The destroyer USS *Sutherland* is damaged after coming under fire off the east coast of Korea.

The actress Celia Imrie (*The Best Exotic Marigold Hotel*) is born in Guildford, Surrey.

Wednesday 16: The UN presents a mediation plan to end the dispute between Pakistan and India over Kashmir.

July 1952

Thursday 17: The actor David Hasselhoff (*Knight Rider, Baywatch*) is born in Baltimore, Maryland.

Soviet diplomat Pavel Kuznetov is expelled from Britain following espionage allegations.

Marilyn Monroe in *Don't Bother to Knock.*

Friday 18: The thriller film *Don't Bother to Knock*, starring Richard Widmark and Marilyn Monroe is released.

Saturday 19: The 1952 Summer Olympics begins in Helsinki, Finland.

Sunday 20: The foundation stone of Berlin's memorial to the German (anti-Hitler) resistance in the Second World War is laid.

Monday 21: 12 people are killed when a 7.3 earthquake hits Kern County, California.

Tuesday 22: The International Court of Justice rules that Britain's colonial control of Iranian oilfields is no longer justifiable. The decision leads to a UK/US boycott of Iran.

Wednesday 23: King Farouk of Egypt is overthrown in a coup led by General Mohammed Naguib.

Thursday 24: The western film *High Noon* starring Gary Cooper is released.

David Hasselhoff is born on 17 July.

In the Helsinki olympics, Czech runner Emil Zatopek sets a world record for the marathon at 2.23.03.

Friday 25: Puerto Rico becomes a self-governing commonwealth of the United States.

Gary Cooper stars in the classic western film *High Noon*, released on 24 July.

Saturday 26: Eva Peron, the first lady of Argentina, dies aged 33.

Sunday 27: One Portuguese soldier is killed and 13 injured when troops come under fire from Red Chinese forces in a border skirmish with Portugal's Macau colony.

Eva Peron dies on 26 July.

Monday 28: 12 ships of Britain's Mediterranean fleet are despatched from Malta to Egypt for peacekeeping duties following the abdication of King Farouk.

Tuesday 29: On the final day of the 17-day spate of UFO sightings in Washington, DC, 12 unidentified flying objects are reported over the US capital.

Wednesday 30: The future South African president Nelson Mandela is arrested in connection with his role in the Defiance Campaign against apartheid.

Thursday 31: The Swedish humanitarian Raoul Wallenberg, who saved thousands of Jews from the Holocaust, is believed to have died on this day in Soviet captivity.

August
1952

Friday 1: All US forces in Europe are brought under the unified authority of US European Command (USEUCOM).

Saturday 2: US boxer Floyd Patterson wins Olympic gold after his knock-out of Romania's Vasile Tita.

Sunday 3: Italy's Alberto Ascari wins the 1952 Formula One World Drivers' Championship.

The 1952 Summer Olympics closes.

Monday 4: The People's Republic of China football team

F1 champ Alberto Ascari.

plays its first international match, losing 4-0 to Finland, one of the few countries to recognise Mao's communist regime.

Tuesday 5: Syngman Rhee becomes President of South Korea.

The Treaty of Tapei between the Republic of China and Japan formally ends the Second Sino-Japanese War (1937-1945).

King Hussein accedes to the throne of Jordan on 11 August, aged 16.

Wednesday 6: Russia's Vladimir Kuntsevich sets the world high jump record at 1.81m (5'9.3").

Thursday 7: UN observers are placed on alert as Greek troops fire on Bulgarian forces sighted on the border island of Gamma.

The comedian Alexei Sayle (*The Young Ones*) is born in Liverpool, England.

Friday 8: Commander Peter 'Hoagy' Carmichael, Royal Navy, becomes the only pilot in the Korean War to shoot down a jet fighter (MiG-15) while flying a piston aircraft (Hawker Sea Fury).

Saturday 9: The historic novelist Jeffery Farnol, pioneer of the Regency romance genre, dies aged 74.

Sunday 10: Communist forces fire over 20,000 rounds of artillery in a heavy counter-attack against Allied forces in Korea known as the Battle of Bunker Hill.

Monday 11: Aged just 16, King Hussein of Jordan accedes to the throne, following the abdication of his father King Talal on health grounds.

Tuesday 12: 13 Soviet Jews are executed in Moscow for counter-revolutionary crimes.

The 17 year old King Faisal of Iraq arrives in the USA for a state visit.

Wednesday 13: US Marines repulse the Communist counter-attack in Korea, defending the key territory of Bunker Hill against several large-scale infantry charges.

Japan joins the International Monetary Fund (IMF).

August 1952

King Faisal of Iraq, 17, begins a US tour on 12 August.

Thursday 14: West Germany joins the IMF and the World Bank.

Friday 15: Britain's eleven-day Operation Cumulus experiment to 'seed' clouds with chemicals to provoke rainfall ends.

Saturday 16: 34 people are killed in flash floods when nine inches of rain fall in 24 hours on the village of Lynmouth in Devon, south-east England. No link with Operation Cumulus (*see above*) is ever proved, but suspicions remain.

Sunday 17: The Formula One champion racing driver Nelson Piquet born in Rio de Janeiro, Brazil.

Monday 18: The actor Patrick Swayze is born in Houston, Texas (died 2009).

Tuesday 19: Patrick Hamilton's pre-war theatrical smash hit *Gaslight* (US title: *Angel Street*) is revived off-Broadway.

Wednesday 20: The prototype of the RAF Gloster Javelin night fighter makes its first flight.

Left: the RAF Gloster Javelin jet fighter.

August 1952

Thursday 21: Joe Strummer, lead singer of The Clash is born in Ankara, Turkey (died 2002).

Friday 22: Two people are killed and damage worth $10m is caused when a severe earthquake hits Bakersfield, California.

Saturday 23: Soviet premier Joseph Stalin sends his final 'Stalin Note' to the Allied powers in West Germany offering to negotiate German re-unification; his proposals are rejected.

Joe Strummer is born on 21 August.

The Bristol Belvedere first flies on 24 August.

Sunday 24: Britain's Bristol Belvedere helicopter, the first helicopter for commercial and passenger use, makes its maiden flight.

Monday 25: US Presidential candidate Dwight D Eisenhower makes a radio address in support of the Korean War, in which he states 'never shall we rest complete until the tidal mud of aggressive communism has receded within its own borders.'

Tuesday 26: The first non-stop there-and-back crossing of the Atlantic by jet plane is made, when an English Electric Canberra bomber completes the trip in 10 hours 3 minutes.

August 1952

Wednesday 27: The comedian Paul Reubens (Pee-Wee Herman) is born in Peekskill, New York.

Thursday 28: NATO countries sign the Paris Protocol, which establishes military headquarters in all member states.

Friday 29: The premiere of avant-garde composer John Cage's *4'33"* takes place in Woodstock, New York. The piece consists of four minutes and thirty-three seconds of total silence.

Saturday 30: The prototype RAF Avro Vulcan bomber makes its first flight.

Sunday 31: 13 people are killed in a crash on West Germany's Grenzlandring racetrack, after which the track is permanently closed.

Left: the RAF Avro Vulcan jet bomber.

September
1952

Monday 1: Ernest Hemingway's novel *The Old Man and the Sea* is published.

Tuesday 2: Doctors C Walton Lillehei and F John Lewis perform the first open heart surgery, at the University of Minnesota.

Ernest Hemingway.

Wednesday 3: Mahmood Hussein Mattan is hanged for the murder of Lily Volpert in Cardiff, Wales. 45 years later he is posthumously pardoned and his family receive £725,000 compensation, the first such award for a person wrongfully hanged.

Thursday 4: One policeman is killed and another seriously injured when an armed embezzler, Edwin Finlay, shoots them during an arrest attempt in Hyndland Road, Glasgow. A third unarmed constable manages to draw Finlay's fire until reinforcements arrive, at which point Finlay takes his own life.

Friday 5: John Howard Godar, 31, is hanged for the murder of his girlfriend Maureen Cox, 20, in a taxi in Uxbridge, Middlesex in June 1952.

September 1952

**US tennis champion
Maureen Connolly.**

US commanders in Korea announce that communist troop levels in the country have now reached one million.

Saturday 6: Farnborough disaster: 31 people are killed when a DH 110 aeroplane crashes into the crowd at Farnborough Air Show in southern England.

Television broadcasting begins in Canada.

Sunday 7: US Army researchers claim the recent spate of 'UFO' sightings could be atmospheric phenomena.

Monday 8: Frank Sedgman and Maureen Connolly win the US National Championships tennis tournament.

Tuesday 9: Musician and producer Dave Stewart of the Eurythmics is born in Sunderland.

Wednesday 10: Seven communist planes are shot down and 12 damaged during aerial clashes with UN forces over North Korea.

The aircraft carriers USS *Wright*, HMS *Illustrious* and HMS *Eagle* in convoy as part of Operation Mainbrace.

September 1952

The first session of the European Parliament is held.

West Germany agrees to pay war reparations to Israel.

Jo Stafford tops the charts on 13 September.

Thursday 11: King Hailie Sellassie of Ethopia signs the country's act of union with Eritrea.

Friday 12: Noel Coward's play *Quadrille* opens at the Phoenix Theatre, London.

Saturday 13: *You Belong to Me* by Jo Stafford hits number one in the US singles charts.

Sunday 14: Pope Pius XII declares that support for the death penalty is compatible with Roman Catholic belief.

The first large scale NATO naval exercise, Operation Mainbrace, begins in the North Atlantic.

Monday 15: Britain's Foreign Secretary Anthony Eden becomes the first British politician to address the newly formed Council of Europe.

Tuesday 16: The actor Mickey Rourke (*Angel Heart*) is born in Schenectady, New York.

Wednesday 17: A typhoon devastates Wake Island in Hawaii, causing 750 people to be made homeless.

Thursday 18: Japan's application to join the United Nation is vetoed by the USSR.

Mickey Rourke is born on 16 September.

September 1952

US troops unload timber to build defences on 'Old Baldy' in Korea.

Friday 19: Following a trip to England, Charlie Chaplin is barred from re-entering the USA for his alleged communist sympathies.

Saturday 20: A major Chinese infantry attack drives UN allied forces off the key defensive hill nicknamed 'Old Baldy' near Panmunjom, Korea.

Rocky Marciano.

Sunday 21: British business magnate Sir Montague Burton, founder of the Burton menswear chain, dies aged 67.

Monday 22: A savage counter-attack by UN allied forces recaptures the strategic 'Old Baldy' hill in Korea.

Tuesday 23: Rocky Marciano wins the World Heavyweight boxing title when he knocks out Jersey Joe Walcott in Philadelphia.

Wednesday 24: The Kentucky Fried Chicken chain is founded by Colonel Harlan Sanders.

The French submarine *La Sibyll* is lost with all hands in a diving accident off the coast near Toulon.

Thursday 25: Actor Christopher Reeve is born in New York City (died 2004).

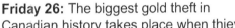

Christopher Reeve.

Friday 26: The biggest gold theft in Canadian history takes place when thieves take half a ton of bullion (worth US$356,000) from Malton Airport in Toronto.

Saturday 27: The romantic novelist Katie Fforde is born in London, England.

Sunday 28: The USSR rejects proposals by the western Allies to restore sovereignty to Austria, occupied since 1945.

Monday 29: Three times world land speed record holder John Cobb is killed while attempting to break the world water speed record on Loch Ness, Scotland.

Tuesday 30: The Revised Standard Version of the Bible, the first major English translation since the 17th century, is published.

October
1952

Wednesday 1: 45 Chinese POWs are killed during rioting in Cheju Island allied prison camp, Korea.

Thursday 2: Large-scale celebrations take place across mainland China to mark the third anniversary of the communist uprising.

Friday 3: In Operation Hurricane, the first British nuclear bomb is detonated in the Monte Bello Islands, Australia.

Britain's first atomic bomb is detonated in Western Australia on 3 October.

Saturday 4: The British trawler *Norman* is lost off the coast of Greenland with 19 hands; only one crew member survives.

Britain's second worst rail disaster happens on 8 October at Harrow and Wealdstone near London.

Sunday 5: Wartime tea rationing ends in the United Kingdom.

Monday 6: The Korean War film *Retreat, Hell!* is released.

Tuesday 7: Russian President Vladimir Putin is born in Leningrad.

The New York Yankees defeat the Brooklyn Dodgers to win baseball's World Series.

Wednesday 8: 112 people are killed and 340 injured when three trains collide at Harrow and Wealdstone station near London. It remains the second deadliest rail disaster in British history.

Russian premier Vladimir Putin is born on 7 October.

Thursday 9: TV personality Sharon Osbourne is born in London, England.

Friday 10: Fierce hand-to-hand combat takes place on White Horse Mountain, Korea. Possession of the territory changes five times in one night between UN Allied forces and communists.

October 1952

The UN building opens on 14 October.

Saturday 11: An outbreak of encephalitis in California is declared over, with a total of 47 deaths.

Sunday 12: Further desperate fighting takes place on White Horse Mountain in Korea, with the strategic point changing hands 23 times in 115 hours of non-stop combat.

Monday 13: One man is killed and two injured when an RAF Wellington bomber crashes on manoeuvres near Lichfield, Staffordshire.

Tuesday 14: The United Nations headquarters building in New York City opens.

Wednesday 15: EB White's bestselling children's book *Charlotte's Web* is first published.

Thursday 16: The Charlie Chaplin comedy-drama film *Limelight* premieres in London.

Friday 17: An attempted military coup takes place in Jakarta, Indonesia.

Saturday 18: The US satirical publication *Mad Magazine* is first issued.

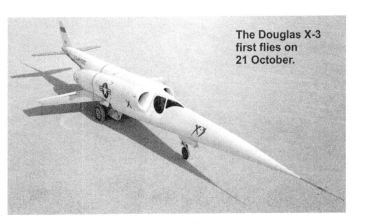

The Douglas X-3 first flies on 21 October.

Sunday 19: In order to prove human endurance, dietician Alain Bombard begins a crossing of the Atlantic in a small open dinghy without food or water. He survives the 65 day voyage by catching fish, and drinking rainwater and small amounts of seawater.

John Bamford, aged 15, rescues his two brothers from a house fire in Newthorpe, Nottinghamshire. He becomes the youngest person to receive the George Cross for civilian bravery.

Monday 20: Martial law is declared in Kenya following the Mau Mau uprising.

The actor Basil Radford (Chalders and Caldicott) dies aged 55.

Tuesday 21: The US air force announces a succesful test flight of its new X3 Douglas *Stiletto* plane, capable of reaching speeds of 1,238mph.

Wednesday 22: The actor Jeff Goldblum is born in West Homestead, Pennsylvania.

Thursday 23: James W Montee, the USA's oldest licenced pilot, celebrates his 90th birthday by taking 40 friends and relatives for a flight over Los Angeles.

Jeff Goldblum.

October 1952

French troops question a suspected communist guerilla in Vietnam.

Friday 24: 443 people are killed when a typhoon hits Luzon in the Philippines.

Saturday 25: Major clashes take place between colonial French forces and Vietminh communist guerillas in Vietnam.

Sunday 26: Professor Sir Andrew Motion, Poet Laureate (1999-2009) is born in London.

Monday 27: The musical comedy film *Because You're Mine,* starring Mario Lanza, receives its Royal Premiere in London.

Tuesday 28: The Douglas XA3-D Skywarrior makes its first flight, from Edwards Air Force base, California.

Wednesday 29: Fierce close-quarter fighting takes place in Korea as UN Allied forces regain Sniper Ridge.

Thursday 30: The Soviet Foreign minister Andrei Vishinsky calls for a UN commission to end the Korean War.

Friday 31: The actress Jane Wymark (*Midsomer Murders*) is born in London.

November
1952

Saturday 1: In Operation Ivy, the first US hydrogen bomb is detonated at Eniwetok Atoll.

Sunday 2: Christopher Craig, 16, shoots dead an unarmed police constable who interrupts him and friend Derek Bentley, 19, while robbing a warehouse in Croydon, near London. Under the law of joint enterprise, Bentley is later sentenced to death because Craig is too young to hang. The case becomes a *cause célèbre* for the revocation of the death penalty in England.

US Presidential and Vice-Presidential candidates Eisenhower and Nixon (Republican) take a break from the election campaign trail.

November 1952

The defeated US Presidential candidate, Adlai Stevenson (Democrat), is snapped while displaying a hole in his shoe. 'Better a hole in the shoe than a hole in the head' is his response to critics.

Monday 3: US Presidential candidate Adlai Stevenson (Democratic) announces that the Korean War is a 'test case' against the global spread of communism.

Tuesday 4: General Dwight D Eisenhower (Republican) wins the 1952 US Presidential Election.

2,300 are killed when a violent earthquake and tsunami hits Kamchatka, USSR.

Wednesday 5: Following his defeat in the US Presidential Election, Adlai Stevenson urges the nation to unite behind Eisenhower.

Thursday 6: In the UN Security Council the British representative, Sir Gladwyn Jebb, calls for a plebiscite on the disputed Indian/Pakistani territory of Kashmir.

Friday 7: US President Truman and President-Elect Eisenhower agree to talks on ending the Korean War.

Trygve Lie, UN Secretary General, resigns on 10 November.

Saturday 8: HM Queen Elizabeth attends her first Festival of Remembrance at the Albert Hall, London.

Sunday 9: Chaim Weizmann, first President of Israel (1949-1952) dies aged 77.

Monday 10: Trygve Lie resigns as first Secretary-General of the United Nations following complaints from Soviet and US sources over his handling of the Korean War.

Tuesday 11: The Soviet Tupolev Tu-95 heavy bomber makes its first flight.

Wednesday 12: Actress Joan Fontaine marries actor Collier Young.

Thursday 13: The actor Art Malik (*The Jewel in the Crown*) is born in Bahawalpur, Pakistan.

A huge manhunt begins in Northern Ireland after Patricia Curran, 19, the daughter of a High Court judge, is found murdered.

Friday 14: The magazine *New Musical Express* publishes the first UK singles chart. *Here In My Heart* by Al Martino is announced as the first British number one single.

Above left: Joan Fontaine
Left: Al Martino, first singer to top the UK music charts.

November 1952

Saturday 15: French author René Belbenoît, following a successful escape from the French prison colony of Devil's Island, is granted leave to remain in the USA.

Sunday 16: The US Department of Agriculture announces that improved harvests have led to wartime rationing ending in nearly all countries.

Monday 17: Cyril Ramaphosa, President of South Africa (2018-), is born in Johannesburg.

Tuesday 18: A US military C-119 'flying boxcar' transporter plane crashes in California with the loss of eight lives; it is the fourth such aircraft to crash in 11 days.

Wednesday 19: The Second Battle of the Hook in Korea ends in UN Allied victory.

Thursday 20: American Ufologist George Adamski claims that he has met an alien named Orthon who landed in a flying saucer in the Colorado Desert. Sceptics claim Adamski's photograph of the 'flying saucer' is actually of a lamp used for brooding chickens.

The Japanese Peace Bell, presented to the United Nations in 1954 as a symbol of reconciliation after the Second World War, is cast on 24 November.

The world's **FIRST FEATURE LENGTH** motion picture in NATURAL VISION

arch Oboler's **3 DIMENSION** "**BWANA DEVIL**" in Thrilling COLOR

A LION in your lap!

ARCH OBOLER'S "BWANA DEVIL" IN THRILLING COLOR · Starring ROBERT STACK · BARBARA BRITTON · NIGEL BRUCE · Released thru United Artists

Bwana Devil, the first 3D feature film, is released on 26 November. The film is intended to entice the growing numbers of TV viewers back into cinemas.

Friday 21: The RAF Percival Pembroke transporter plane makes its first flight.

Saturday 22: 52 people are killed when a Douglas C-124 Globemaster plane crashes in the Chugach Mountains, Alaska.

Sunday 23: Communist Vietminh forces begin besieging the French fortress of Nasan, Vietnam.

Monday 24: The Japanese Peace Bell memorial, donated to the United Nations headquarters in 1954, is cast.

Tuesday 25: *The Mousetrap* by Agatha Christie opens at the New Ambassadors Theatre in London. It becomes the world's longest running play, with over 27,000 performances by 2020.

Wednesday 26: The first 3D feature film, *Bwana Devil*, is released in the USA.

Thursday 27: 16 people die in extreme cold weather across themidwest USA; heavy snowfalls reach as far south as Texas.

Friday 28: The first pillar box of Queen Elizabeth II's reign is installed in Scotland. The following day it is defaced and

November 1952

eventually blown up by nationalists angered that it bears the 'E II R' cypher, considered incorrect since Elizabeth the First never reigned in Scotland.

Saturday 29: US President-Elect Dwight D Eisenhower begins a tour of Korea.

Sunday 30: Communist China rejects UN proposals for ending the Korean War, aligning itself instead with a Soviet plan.

December 1952

Monday 1: *The New York Times* announces that Christine (formerly George) Jorgensen has become the first American to undergo a sex-change operation.

Tuesday 2: Nelson Mandela is charged under South Africa's Suppression of Communism Act and sentenced to nine months hard labour, suspended for two years.

Wednesday 3: The USSR rejects UN Allied proposals for peace talks in Korea, pushing instead for an immediate ceasefire.

The four-day Great Smog begins in London on 4 December.

December 1952

Thursday 4: The four-day Great Smog of 1952 begins in London. The event leads to the banning of coal and wood burning in most urban areas by 1956.

Friday 5: 18 American UN employees are fired after being found to have links to communist organisations.

President-Elect Eisenhower departs from Korea, narrowly avoiding the largest aerial attack of the war so far.

Yitzhak Ben-Zvi becomes President of Israel on 8 December.

Saturday 6: Charles Salvador (formerly Charles Bronson) is born in Luton, Bedfordshire. He is dubbed 'Britain's most notorious prisoner' after conviction for violent armed robbery in the 1970s.

Sunday 7: Construction begins on the memorial to the 2000 US servicemen who lost their lives in the 1941 attack on Pearl Harbor.

Monday 8: Yitzhak Ben-Zvi wins the Israeli presidential election.

Major talks on the future of US policy in Korea and the far east take place on board USS *Helena* near Hawaii.

Bill and Ben the Flowerpot Men first appear on BBC TV on 12 December.

Tuesday 9: Over 50 people are killed in clashes between arab nationalists and French colonial forces in Casablanca, Morocco.

London's Great Smog ends with over 4,000 dead from respiratory illness exacerbated by the severe pollution.

Wednesday 10: Britain's Archer Martin and Richard Synge win the Nobel Prize for Chemistry, for their invention of partition chromatography.

Thursday 11: The US Army launches nylon body armour for use by soldiers in Korea.

Friday 12: The BBC TV children's puppet show *Flowerpot Men*, featuring 'Bill and Ben', is first broadcast.

Saturday 13: Representatives of European states meet at the Paris Conference in order to devise a system of pan-European healthcare.

Chromatography scientist Richard Synge. Along with Archer Martin he is awarded the Nobel Prize for Chemistry on 10 December.

Sunday 14: The first successful separation of siamese twins takes place at Mount Sinai Hospital, Cleveland, Ohio.

Monday 15: The Soviet submarine S-117 is lost with all hands in the Sea of Japan.

The Sands Hotel casino opens in Las Vegas, making $285,000 in the first six hours of gaming.

Tuesday 16: 82 communist POWs are killed during a mass break-out of prisoners from Pongam Island prison camp, Korea.

December 1952

Poster for the gala opening of the Sands Hotel, Las Vegas, 15 December.

Wednesday 17: Admiral the Earl Mountbatten is named as supreme commander of NATO's Mediterranean fleet.

The government of Yugoslavia severs diplomatic relations with the Vatican.

Thursday 18: William Morris, Lord Nuffield, retires as head of the British Motor Corporation.

Friday 19: A deranged man is caught by a police dog after invading the grounds of Buckingham Palace, London.

Saturday 20: Lawyers for the actress Marilyn Monroe announce a clampdown on unlicensed products bearing her image, with a $15 tray featuring her in the nude being one of the best sellers.

86 US servicemen are killed when a C-124 Globemaster transporter plane crashes in Moses Lake, WA.

Sunday 21: Television broadcasting begins in East Germany.

The French actress Brigitte Bardot, 18, marries film director Roger Vadim, 27.

Monday 22: The exiled Duke of Windsor, formerly King Edward VIII, announces he will not attend the coronation of his niece Queen Elizabeth II.

Tuesday 23: Evangelist Billy Graham, serving as a forces chaplain on board the hospital ship Jutlandia, urges Americans to pray for peace in Korea.

December 1952

Wednesday 24: Dr Alain Bombard completes his solo crossing of the Atlantic by open dinghy, surviving on a diet of fish and rainwater.

Thursday 25: HM Queen Elizabeth II delivers her first Christmas radio broadcast to the Commonwealth.

Friday 26: Sovier leader Josef Stalin calls for a peace conference to end the Korean War.

Saturday 27: The Japanese government donates the summit of Mount Fuji to be used as a religious shrine.

Lord Mountbatten becomes supreme commander of NATO's Mediterranean Fleet on 17 December.

Sunday 28: A second deadly smog hits Britain, this time resulting in fewer fatalities, but spread over a wider area.

A US Army report describes the war in Korea as the worst stalemate since the First World War, with almost no territory gained in over a year of fighting.

Monday 29: It is reported that a second example of the ancient Ceolocanth fish, thought long extinct, has been found off the coast of Madgascar.

Tuesday 30: A negligent bridge watchman opens the cantilevers of Tower Bridge, London, while a double-decker bus is crossing. The quick thinking driver, Albert Gunter, accelerates rapidly and jumps the bus over the gap, saving the passengers from almost certain death and breaking his leg in the process. For this bravery he is awarded £10 and a day off work.

Wednesday 31: British Prime Minister Winston Churchill sails to New York for Korean War talks with US President Elect Eisenhower.

Other titles from Montpelier Publishing:

A Little Book of Limericks:
Funny Rhymes for all the Family
ISBN 9781511524124

Scottish Jokes: A Wee Book of
Clean Caledonian Chuckles
ISBN 9781495297366

The Old Fashioned Joke Book:
Gags and Funny Stories
ISBN 9781514261989

Non-Religious Funeral Readings:
Philosophy and Poetry for Secular
Services
ISBN 9781500512835

Large Print Jokes: Hundreds of
Gags in Easy-to-Read Type
ISBN 9781517775780

**Spiritual Readings for Funerals
and Memorial Services**
ISBN 9781503379329

Victorian Murder: True Crimes,
Confessions and Executions
ISBN 9781530296194

Large Print Prayers: A Prayer for
Each Day of the Month
ISBN 9781523251476

**A Little Book of Ripping Riddles
and Confounding Conundrums**
ISBN 9781505548136

Vinegar uses: over 150 ways to use
vinegar
ISBN 9781512136623

Large Print Wordsearch:
100 Puzzles in Easy-to-Read Type
ISBN 9781517638894

The Pipe Smoker's Companion
ISBN 9781500441401

The Book of Church Jokes
ISBN 9781507620632

Bar Mitzvah Notebook
ISBN 9781976007781

Jewish Jokes
ISBN 9781514845769

Large Print Address Book
ISBN 9781539820031

How to Cook Without a Kitchen:
Easy, Healthy and Low-Cost Meals
9781515340188

Large Print Birthday Book
ISBN 9781544670720

Retirement Jokes
ISBN 9781519206350

Take my Wife: Hilarious Jokes of
Love and Marriage
ISBN 9781511790956

Welsh Jokes: A Little Book of
Wonderful Welsh Wit
ISBN 9781511612241

1001 Ways to Save Money: Thrifty
Tips for the Fabulously Frugal!
ISBN 9781505432534

Available online at Amazon

Printed in Great Britain
by Amazon